D1546908

ANOTHER PERIOD IN
COIN COLLECTING

Margaret Amstell is well-known to hundreds of coin collectors. She has been a professional numismatist for many years with Seaby's, one of Europe's foremost coin dealers. Her particular interest is in ancient and modern gold coins of the world, but she is also a student of the silver coinage of the British Isles.

The coins of England, and particularly the ones covered by her book, provide a wonderful portrait gallery of the reigning Monarchs, and they are, of course, by the best contemporary artists.

ANOTHER PERIOD IN COIN COLLECTING

English Coins

CHARLES I TO EDWARD III

Introduction to the Hammered Coinage

MARGARET AMSTELL

LONDON

W. FOULSHAM & CO. LTD.

[1967]

NEW YORK   TORONTO   CAPE TOWN   SYDNEY

W. FOULSHAM & CO. LTD.

Yeovil Road, Slough, Bucks., England

572-00448-6

© *Copyright* W. FOULSHAM AND CO. LTD. 1967

Made and printed in Great Britain by

WILLMER BROTHERS LIMITED, BIRKENHEAD

You may live without poetry, music and art;
You may live without conscience and live without heart;
You may live without friends; you may live without drawings,
But civilized man cannot live without coins.

(with apologies to the Earl of Lytton)

Dedicated to A.D.A.

ACKNOWLEDGEMENTS

All the photographs were taken by P. Frank Purvey from coins kindly loaned by B. A. Seaby Ltd.

I should like to record my thanks to Frank Purvey for the willing help he gave me with the proofs.

M.A.

Introduction

Again, I ask myself what *is* it that makes coins so fascinating?
Is it their close alliance to art, to sculpture, to design? Is it
because they are practically indestructible and yet portable? Is it,
perhaps, their power to stimulate our curiosity? Via coins, I have
needed to investigate:—

(1) Engineering

(2) Geography

(3) Metallurgy

(4) Lettering

(5) Heraldry

(6) Economics

(7) Politics

(8) Theology

(9) Language

(10) Costume

(11) Architecture, and of course

(12) History

Some knowledge of all these subjects comes to one just as a
by-product of the pursuit of numismatics. There must be few
things (if any) more satisfying to collect than coins.

Pope must have been attacked by the coin 'bug' when he
wrote:—

'Ambition sighed; she found it vain to trust
The faithless column, and the crumbling bust,
Huge moles, whose shadow stretched from shore to shore,
Their ruins perished, and their place no more!
Convinced, she now contracts her vast design,
And all her triumphs shrink into a coin.'

A Selection of Numismatic Information

The letter 'Z' on many coins is an ancient contraction for 'ET'. The letter 'E' was often used for the diphthong 'AE'.

*　　*　　*

Mintmark (sometimes written mm.) was originally used to show where the legend began. Later this mark (before the dating of coins) indicated the period of striking and, later still, the mint where the coin was struck.

*　　*　　*

Countermark (sometimes written Cmk.). This was a mark stamped into a coin, usually to alter its value and/or place of circulation.

*　　*　　*

Restrike. This is a coin struck from the original dies at a date later than that of the original issue.

*　　*　　*

Tooling. This is an attempt to 'improve' a coin by deepening some of the outlines with an engraving tool.

*　　*　　*

Brockage. This is caused by a flan getting stuck in the machine in the striking; another blank then comes between the upper and lower die and the first piece impresses its design on the second, at the moment of impact. Unlike stamps, (where freaks are much sought after) there are not many collectors of brockages since perfection is the aim of most coin collectors.

9

Electrotypes. These are copies made in two halves and then joined with solder. They are not made to deceive, but to help students and also for display. They are easily detected as it is impossible to conceal the join.

* * *

Piedford. This is a coin struck on a thicker blank than usual.

* * *

Ligate. When letters are joined together thus Æ they are said to be 'ligate'.

Legends and Mottoes

OBVERSE

EDWARDVS
HENRICVS
RICARDVS
HENRICVS VIII
} *Dei Gratia, Rex Angliae et Franciae Dominus Hiberniae*
(By the grace of God, King of England and France, Lord of Ireland)

HENRICVS VIII
EDWARD VI
} *Rutilans Rosa Sine Spina*
(the shining rose without a thorn)

HENRICVS 8 or VIII
EDWARDVS 6 or VI
MARIA
ELIZABETHA
} *Dei Gratia, Angliae, Franciae, et Hiberniae Rex (or Regina)*
(By the grace of God, King (or Queen) of England, France and Ireland)

PHILLIPVS et MARIA   DEI GRATIA REX et REGINA
By the grace of God, King and Queen

JACOBVS   DEI GRATIA, ANGLIAE, SCOTIAE, FRANCIAE, et HIBERNIAE, REX
By the grace of God, King of England, Scotland, France and Ireland

J.D.G. ROSA SINE SPINA = James, by the grace of God, a rose without a thorn

JACOBVS
CAROLVS
} DEI GRATIA, MAGNAE BRITANNIAE, FRANCIAE et HIBERNIAE REX
By the grace of God, King of Great Britain, France and Ireland

OLIVARIVS   DEI GRATIA REIPVBLICAE ANGLIAE, SCOTIAE et HIBERNIAE, PROTECTOR
By the grace of God, Protector of the Republic of England, Scotland and Ireland

REVERSE

The legends and mottoes which appear on the reverses of the coins covered by this volume recur from reign to reign. Therefore they are given here alphabetically with a note following stating the reigns in which they appear.

A DOMINO FACTVM EST ISTVD, ET EST MIRABILE IN OCVLIS NOSTRIS

This is the work of the Lord and is wonderful in our eyes
  (Edward III, Mary, Philip & Mary, Elizabeth I and James I)

AMOR POPVLI PRAESIDIVM REGIS

The love of the people is the King's protection
  (Charles I)

CHRISTO AVSPICE REGNO

I reign under the auspices of Christ
  (Charles I)

CVLTORES SVI DEVS PROTEGIT

God protects his worshippers
  (Charles I)

DOMINE NE IN FVRORE TVO ARGVAS ME

O Lord, rebuke me not in thine anger (Psalm vi, 1)
  (Edward III, Richard II, Henry IV, V & VI, Edward IV)

EXALTABITVR IN GLORIA

He shall be exalted in glory (Psalm cxii, 9)
  (Edward III, Richard II, Henry IV & V, Edward IV & VI)

EXVRGAT DEVS, DISSIPENTVR INIMICI

Let God arise, let his enemies be scattered (Psalm lxviii, 1)
  (James I and Charles I)

FACIAM EOS IN GENTEM VNAM

I will make them one people (Ezekiel xxxvii, 22)
  (James I, alluding to England and Scotland)

FLORENT CONCORDIA REGNA

Kingdoms flourish by concord
  (Charles I)

HENRICVS ROSAS, REGNA JACOBVS

Henry, the roses: James, the Kingdoms
  (James I, alluding to the union of roses of York and Lancaster and the projected union of England and Scotland)

INIMICOS EJVS INDVAM CONFVSIONE
His enemies will I clothe with shame (Psalm cxxxii, 18)
 (Edward VI)

JESVS AVTEM TRANSIENS PER MEDIVM ILLORVM IBAT
But Jesus, passing through the midst of them, went His way
(Luke iv, 30)
 (Edward III, Richard II, Henry IV & V, Edward IV, Henry
 VII & VIII, Edward VI and Elizabeth I)

JVSTITA THRONVM FIRMAT
Justice strengthens a throne
 (Charles I)

LVCERNA PEDIBVS MEIS VERBVM TVVM
Thy word is the light of my footsteps (Psalm cxix, 105)
 (Edward VI)

O CRVX, AVE, SPES VNICA
Hail! O cross, the only hope (hymn, Vexilla Regis)
 (Edward IV, Henry VII & VIII)

PAX QUÆ RITVR BELLO
Peace is to be sought by war
 (Cromwell)

PER CRVCEM TVAM SALVA NOS CHRISTE REDEMPTOR
By thy cross save us, O Christ, our Redeemer
 (Henry VI, restored, Edward IV & V, Richard III, Henry
 VII & VIII, Edward VI)

POSVI DEVM ADJVTOREM MEVM
I have made God my helper (Psalm liv, 4)
 (Edward III, Henry IV, Edward IV, Richard III, Henry VII
 & VIII, Edward VI, Philip & Mary, Elizabeth I)

QUÆ DEVS CONJVNXIT NEMO SEPARET
What God hath joined together, let no man put asunder
(Matthew xix, 6)
 (James I, alluding to the union of Scotland and England)

RELIG. PROT. LEGES. ANGL. LIBER. PARL. (RELIGIO PROTESTANTIVM
LEGES ANGLIÆ LIBERTAS PARLIAMENT)
The religion of the Protestants, the laws of England, the liberty
of Parliament
 (Charles I, alluding to his declaration to preserve these things)

SCVTEM FIDEI PROTEGET EVM or EAM
The shield of faith protects him (or her)
(Edward VI, Elizabeth I)

TALI DICATA SIGNO MENS FLVCTVARE NEQVIT
With such a sign (the cross) a devoted mind is unable to waver
(from a Fourth Century hymn by Prudentius)
(Henry VIII)

TIMOR DOMINI FONS VITE (for VITÆ)
The fear of the Lord is the fountain of life (Proverbs xiv, 27)
(Edward VI)

TVEATUR VNITA DEVS
May God protect the united
(James I and Charles I)

VERITAS TEMPORIS FILIA
Truth is the daughter of Time
(Mary)

A brief description of how coins are made

This volume is concerned with coins struck prior to 1660 going back to 1327 most of which, with certain exceptions (i.e. milled coins struck under Cromwell and Elizabeth I) were struck by hand with a hammer. The apparatus employed was fairly simple, even primitive. With variations and refinements, it would seem that 'hammered' coins were produced by placing hot, soft metal between an upper and lower die and then hammering the upper die until an impression was produced on both sides of the 'flan'.

The underneath die was generally the obverse with the head of the sovereign, and this was made fast in blocks of wood and was known as the *pile* die. The upper die was known as the *trussel* and this was held by hand (or tongs) and then struck. This process continued to be used until the invention of the mill and the screw in 1561. The rolling mill and the screw press, for cutting blanks and striking the coins, were worked by horse and water power. This new method was not, at first, supposed to work well and after being used for about 15 years, side by side with the hammer, it was given up until 1662, when it was finally adopted. The term 'milled' was applied to any coin produced by machinery, and coins so described do not necessarily have a *'milled'* edge (which is correctly called a 'grained' edge).

With the introduction of steam power at the end of the eighteenth century great improvements in minting machinery came into being.

If you wish to see present day methods of coining, a visit to the Royal Mint is recommended. The Royal Mint is (at present) located on Tower Hill, E.C.3 and small parties can be shown around if a prior appointment is made.

The Commonwealth and Oliver Cromwell 1649-1660

On the death of Charles I, Parliament was quick to realise that it would be a good idea to issue coins from which all emblems and portraits of the monarch had been obliterated. All the coins struck during the Commonwealth were made under the hammer and have inscriptions in English instead of Latin. The royal portrait was replaced by the cross of St. George on a plain shield surrounded by a wreath of palm and laurel and the legend reads THE COMMONWEALTH OF ENGLAND, whilst the reverse shows two shields side by side one bearing the cross of St. George and the other the Irish harp with the legend GOD WITH VS and the date. This description applies to the gold and larger coins—the smaller denominations do not have legends (or mint marks).

FIG. 1   Commonwealth crown

FIG. 2   Commonwealth half-groat

The gold coins of the Commonwealth were a unite (20/- piece), (Fig. 3) a double-crown (10/- piece) and a crown (5/- piece). The silver coins consisted of a crown (Fig. 1), half-crown, shilling, sixpence, half-groat (Fig. 2), penny and half-penny (a tiny piece with a single shield on each side). This was the last time a silver half-penny was struck. Most coins of the Commonwealth are rare, but the smaller pieces are often available and consequently are comparatively cheap.

FIG. 3   Commonwealth unite

In 1653 Oliver Cromwell was made Protector of England and he assumed the powers of a dictator. This may account for the portrait on his coins being reminiscent of a Roman emperor, i.e. draped and laurelled (Fig. 4).

It is doubtful if the coins of Cromwell were ever put into circulation. They nearly always turn up in beautiful condition (with the possible exception of half-crowns and shillings) and are generally considered to be patterns.

Cromwell reverted to Latin for his legends (perhaps under the influence of the youthful Milton, who was his Secretary). The obverse inscription on his coins reads OLIVAR D G RP ANG SCO ET HIB &C PRO (Oliver, by the Grace of God, Protector of the Republic of England, Scotland and Ireland, etc.). The reverse legend is PAX QVAERITVR BELLO (Peace is sought by War). It surrounds the crowned arms of the Protectorate in the centre of which on an 'inescutcheon of pretence' is a lion rampant (the personal arms of Cromwell).

B

FIG. 4   Cromwell half-crown

FIG. 5   Cromwell broad

The gold coins consisted of a fifty-shilling piece, a twenty-shilling piece (or broad) (Fig. 5) and a ten-shilling piece (or half-broad). The fifty-shilling piece has on the edge PROTECTOR LITERIS LITERÆ NVMMIS CORONA ET SALVS (A protection for the letters; the letters are a garland and a safeguard to the coinage). The silver coins consist of a crown, half-crown (Fig. 4), shilling, and six-pence. The crown has an edge inscription reading HAS NISI PERITVRVS MIHI ADIMAT NEMO (Let no one remove these [letters] on pain of death). The smaller coins have a grained edge. These coins were made by Blondeau's machine (and belong to the milled series) and they were designed and engraved by the renowned Thomas Simon, one of the finest engravers who ever worked for the London Mint. These were the first coins of modern appearance and the first coins to bear an edge inscription.

The new collector should know that there exist Cromwell crowns that were made from false dies (at a much later date) in the Netherlands. They are known as 'Dutch' crowns. There are also other Cromwell coins which were made from false dies by

John Tanner (who was chief engraver at the mint at the time of George II).

Cromwell seems to have made some attempt to institute a copper currency but the farthings he issued were never put into circulation and are correctly described as patterns. His idea was to replace the tradesmen's tokens (which were a nuisance as they could only be accepted in the district in which the issuer was known) by a regal copper coinage. The idea was never carried out. The majority of the farthings show the draped bust of Cromwell facing left on the obverse and some have a ship under sail, whilst the reverse bore curious legends such as:—'for Necessity of Change'; 'For the Relief of the Poor'; 'Charity and Change' or three columns (for the three Kingdoms) united, and the legend 'Thus United Invincible' around (Fig. 6).

FIG. 6   Cromwell pattern farthing

After Cromwell's death coins were again struck by hand hammering techniques and the more modern machinery of the mill type, introduced by Blondeau, was left unused until after the Restoration (see Vol. I).

Charles I and the Civil War
1625-1649

The reign of Charles I is extremely interesting. It falls into two parts i.e. the years of peace 1625–42 and the years of the civil war, 1642–9. At the beginning of his reign, Charles issued unites, double crowns and British-crowns of 'crown' (22 carat) gold together with angels of 'standard' ($23\frac{1}{2}$ carat) gold from the Tower Mint. The silver coins consisted of crowns, half-crowns, shillings, sixpences, half-groats, pennies and half-pennies.

The angel (which we have not met before) shows St. Michael and the dragon on the obverse with the mark of value (X = 10/–) whilst the reverse depicts a sailing ship and the motto AMOR POPVLI PRAESIDIUM REGIS (the love of the people is the King's protection). At this time the angel was current for 10/–. The angel was often pierced and used as a 'touch' piece. A touch piece is a coin (sometimes a medalet) distributed by the monarch, in the ceremony of healing by touch. They were pierced so that they could be hung round the neck of the sufferer until a cure was effected. Incidentally, Charles I was the last monarch to strike angels.

The main characteristics of Charles I first coinage is a large ruff (see Fig. 7) round the King's neck.

FIG. 7   Charles I shilling. First Coinage with ruff

FIG. 7A   Third coinage sixpence with lace collar

FIG. 8   Charles I half-crown, equestrian type

The large silver (crown and half-crown) is of the equestrian type
i.e. King on horseback (Fig. 8). The reverse of these coins has a
garnished shield of arms and the motto CHRISTO AVSPICE REGNO
(I reign under the auspices of Christ) appears on the silver. Some
of the large silver, shillings and sixpences have 'plumes' above the
shield to denote the Welsh origin of the metal (In 1638 a mint was
established at Aberystwyth). The sixpences bear dates until 1630.

On the gold unites of this issue is found the motto FLORENT
CONCORDIA REGNA (Kingdoms flourish by concord) and CVLTORES
SVI DEVS PROTEGIT (God protects his worshippers) on the half-
unit and gold crown. The smaller silver (two pence and penny)
of this issue have no royal portrait but a crowned rose both sides
on the twopence and uncrowned rose on the penny and half-
penny (Fig. 9A).

FIG. 9   Charles I Tower penny   FIG. 9A   Charles I uncrowned
                                                rose half-penny

Their reverse motto TVEATVR VNITA DEUS (may God protect the united) changed to JUSTITIA THRONVM FIRMAT (justice strengthens a throne). Later the flowers were replaced by a royal portrait on the obverse and a shield on the reverse (Fig. 9).

The above described series displeased his Majesty who had a fine appreciation of art. It was fortunate that Nocolas Briot, a most talented, artistic French die-engraver and medalist, had settled in this country and had become a protégé of the King. In 1628 Briot began to work at Tower Mint and he introduced his machine-struck coins. He established a mill and screw-press although he met with considerable opposition from the staff. Unfortunately, the new machinery could not produce enough coinage to satisfy the demand and so hand-hammering was still carried on. But Briot's milled coinage is very distinctive, and it can easily be recognised by its delicate engraving and perfect roundness in contrast to coins of the first issue. (Fig. 10).

FIG. 10   Briot's half-crown

Briot's coins usually have his initial B in the legend or under the King's bust. Some of his coins (many of which are patterns) are great rarities but the only denomination he does not appear to have struck is the half-penny. Briot was not popular at the Mint and eventually Charles gave him charge of the Scottish Mint which he managed with success. He also prepared many of the fine dies for the Oxford, York, Truro and Weymouth Mints which were established later.

The second issue of the reign depicts Charles with a much smaller ruff and in armour and bore the mint marks cross-on-steps, castle, boar's head, anchor, heart, plume and rose. The second issue crown is a handsome coin similar to the first issue but of better design. The third issue of Charles' coins is distinguished by the royal portrait having no ruff (Fig. 7A) but a lace collar and ribbon of the Garter. This issue started in 1631–2 and continued with some variations until the years of the Civil War.

No regal copper coinage was established but Harrington farthings (Fig. 30) (which will be explained later) remained current and in 1626 a new patent was granted to enable the Duchess of Richmond to strike similar pieces (Fig. 11). In 1634 the patent was bought by Lord Maltravers who continued the striking of farthings until this was stopped in 1644.

After this, tradesmen started making small tokens, mostly in brass, on which their names appeared. They continued to be produced for 20 years or so. They are interesting little pieces and may well appeal to collectors interested in local history with shillings rather than pounds to spend (Fig. 12).

FIG. 11   'Rose' farthing   FIG. 12   17th Century token

FIG. 13   Aberystwyth shilling

The first provincial mint was opened at Aberystwyth in 1638, for the purpose of coining silver from the Welsh mines. A book was the mint mark used for all coins (Fig. 13) of this mint which was closed in 1642 when the mintmaster Thomas Bushell moved to Shrewsbury.

The Shrewsbury Mint remained open for a year only. During this time three new denominations were struck i.e. the gold triple unite (Fig. 14), the large silver pound (Fig. 15) and the half-pound.

FIG. 14   Charles I Oxford triple unite

FIG. 15   Charles I Oxford silver pound

The Shrewsbury Mint also introduced the 'Declaration' reverse (which was also used on many coins of other provincial mints). This reads *RELIG · PROT · LEG · ANG · LIBER · PAR and is found across the field in two lines. It refers to Charles' promise to defend the 'Protestant religion, the liberties of Parliament and the laws of England'. By this time the Civil War had begun.

* Standing for RELIGIO · PROTESTANTIVM · LEGES · ANGLIAE · LIBERTAS · PARLIAMENTI.

The Civil War Coinage 1642-1649

Because of his many quarrels with Parliament the King was forced to quit London in 1642. Parliament came into full possession of Tower Mint but nevertheless allowed the King's name and portrait to be exhibited on the coins issued by their authority until Charles' death in 1649.

FIG. 16   Parliament crown

During the Civil War, Charles struck gold and silver coins at emergency mints including Oxford, Shrewsbury, York, Exeter, Chester, Bristol, Truro, Salisbury, Weymouth, Worcester, Coombe Martin, Lundy and Aberystwyth thus supplying coins for those areas of the country under Royalist control.

During the period 1642–49 coins of the various mints can be identified by their mint marks from the following table:—

Mint	Mintmark		Date	Denominations struck
Tower	(P)	= Parliament	1643	Unite, double-crown, crown,
	(R)	= Parliament	1644	silver crown, half-crown,
	eye	= Parliament	1645	shilling, sixpence, half-
(Fig. 16)	sun	= Parliament	1645	groat, penny
	sceptre	= Parliament	1646–49	

25

Mint	Mintmark	Date	Denominations struck
Bristol	BR monogram ⎫ Plume Pellets Acorn ⎭	1643–46	Unite, half-unite, silver half-crown, shilling, sixpence, groat, threepence, half-groat, penny
Chester	Gerb (wheatsheaf) ⎫ Three gerbs Cinquefoil Plume ⎭	1644–46	Half-crown, threepence
Exeter	Rose Rose & castle Castle ⎫ EX. ⎭	1643–45 1645 1645–46	Silver crown, half-crown, shilling, sixpence, groat, threepence, half-groat, penny

FIG. 17   Charles I Oxford groat

Mint	Mintmark	Date	Denominations struck
Oxford	Plume (with bands) ⎫ Three plumes Pellets ⎭ Plume & OX. ⎫ Lis ⎭	1642–46 1643–46	Triple unite, unite, half-unite, silver pound, half-pound, crown, half-crown, shilling, sixpence, groat, threepence, half-groat, penny
Salisbury or Weymouth or Sandsfoot Castle	Grapes Lis Bird Boar's head Cannon ball Castle cross Helmet Lion Rose Scroll Pear	1643–44	Unite and half-crown, shilling, sixpence, groat, threepence, half-groat
York	Lion	1642–44	Half-crown, shilling, six-pence, threepence
Aberystwyth	Book Plume (N.B.) Coins were struck at this Mint prior to the Civil War i.e. from 1638	1642	Unite, half-crown, shilling, sixpence, groat, threepence, half-groat, penny and half-penny

Mint	Mintmark	Date	Denomination struck
Coombe Martin	Crown	1645–48	Half-crown, shilling, sixpence, groat, threepence, half-groat, penny
Shrewsbury	Plume (without bands)	1642	Triple unite, silver pound, half-pound, crown, half-crown, shilling
Lundy	Plume A = (Appledore or Lundy) B = (Barnstaple or Lundy)	1645–46 1645–46 1646	Half-crown, shilling, sixpence, groat, threepence, half-groat
Truro	Rose Bugle	1642–43	Unite, silver half-pound, crown, half-crown, shilling
Worcester	Pear Three pears	1646	Silver half-crown

After the battle of Edgehill the King moved to Oxford which became his headquarters and mint for the next three years. Bushell moved to Oxford from the Shrewsbury Mint. In 1646 Oxford fell to the Parliamentarians after the mint had produced a large quantity of coins and much of the bullion used came from plate given by the University.

Thomas Bushell also established a mint at Bristol in 1643 and most of the coins struck there are distinguished by the BR monogram. The mint at Truro was established to ensure supplies of coins for the King's followers in the southwest of the country, who were cut off from Oxford. In 1643 the Truro mint was transferred to Exeter. The other mints already mentioned were only open for short periods and there is no absolute certainty that the coins are correctly attributed. There are many coins of this reign which learned numismatists have not yet been able to assign to any particular mint.

Mention must be made of 'siege-pieces'. Following the overthrow of the Royalists at Nazeby the civil war devolved into a succession of sieges. The King's men defended numerous castles throughout the land. Emergency issues were struck at Carlisle, Scarborough, Lathom House, Newark, Colchester and Pontefract in order to pay the defending troops and obtain supplies. The majority of these coins are of crude work as no experienced moneyers were available to produce them. They were struck from roughly shaped fragments of plate (often trays, platters, cups, etc.). Some siege pieces even carry hall marks, or part of the original design of the plate.

The pieces which turn up most frequently are half-crowns, shillings, ninepences and sixpences of Newark. These are all lozenge-shaped (Fig. 18) and were struck between 1645 and 1646.

FIG. 18   Newark shilling

FIG. 19   Pontefract shilling struck in the name of Charles II

On the obverse they show the value in pence surmounted by a large crown with C and R on either side. The reverse is inscribed OBS NEWARK (Newark besieged) and the date.

The main issue of Pontefract consists of shillings (Fig. 19) although two-shillings were also struck. The former is struck from round dies whilst the latter is lozenge-shaped. Some coins were struck at Pontefract in the name of Charles II. All the coins portray Pontefract Castle and those in the name of Charles I have the inscription DVM SPIRO SPERO (Whilst I live I hope). The silver three shillings and shillings of Carlisle are usually round and resemble the Newark coin in type. Only gold half-unites were struck at Colchester Castle and these are extremely rare.

The Scarborough pieces were square, octagonal or rectangular and the value of the coin was decided by the weight of the silver. This resulted in unusual denominations, among them a two-and-tenpence, a two-and-fourpence, a one-and-a-penny and a seven-pence. Some of these pieces have the legend CAROLI FORTVNA RESVRGAM (The fortune of Charles will rise again). There is only one piece known to be struck at Lathom House, a uniface shilling; this odd shaped piece is preserved in the British Museum.

The luckless Charles was brought to trial, and was condemned to death on 27th January, 1649 and three days later was beheaded. If he did nothing else of value, Charles I certainly provided endless joy for numismatists.

James I 1603-1625

James I of England was James VI of Scotland. He was the son of Mary, Queen of Scots and Henry Darnley. One of his first acts on coming to the throne of England was to instruct the then Master of the Tower Mint, Sir Richard Martin, to add the title 'King of Scotland' to the titles on his coins, which now were to read IACOBUS D' G' ANG' SCO' FRAN' ET HIB' REX. A new royal shield was also devised to commemorate the union of the two countries. The shield, which formerly had borne the arms of France in the first and fourth quarters and those of England in the second and third quarters, now bore the arms of England (leopards and lilies) in the first and fourth quarters of the shield,

FIG. 20A   Old and new shields

the rampant lion of Scotland being placed in the second quarter and the Irish harp in the third quarter (Fig. 20A).

The first issue of James included the sovereign, half-sovereign, crown and half-crown all of 'crown' (22 carat) gold. They nearly all have the mint mark thistle. The sovereign shows the King dressed in armour to the waist. He is crowned and holds an orb and sceptre. The reverse has a garnished shield (of the new United Kingdom) between I and R and the legend reads EXVRGAT DEVS DISSIPENTVR INIMICI (let God arise, and let his enemies be scattered). The half-sovereign, crown and half-crown have a smaller portrait (as far as the shoulders only) and are similar to the sovereign except for the legend which reads TVEATVR VNITA DEVS (may God protect the United [Kingdoms]).

The corresponding silver issue consisted of all denominations from the crown to the half-penny (Figs. 20–22) omitting the groat and the threepence. The silver crown and half-crown are handsome coins and both show the King on horseback. The shilling and sixpences have a head and shoulders portrait of the King. All have the EXVRGAT legend. The sixpence was the only coin to bear a date during this reign (Fig. 20). The half-groat and penny

FIG. 20   James I sixpence, 1603

FIG. 21   James I first
coinage penny

FIG. 22   James I first
coinage half-penny

FIG. 23   James I second coinage rose ryal

have a similar bust on the obverse and the legend I' D' G' ROSA
SINE SPINA (James, by the grace of God, a rose without a thorn)
but have no reverse legend. The little half-pennies have the
portcullis obverse and cross with pellets in the angles reverse
with no legend either side (Fig. 22).

FIG. 24   James I second coinage spur ryal

In 1604, James, who took a great interest in his coinage, issued
a proclamation ordering that the title King of Great Britain,
France and Ireland should be used on his coins (MAG' BRIT'
instead of ANG' SCO' etc.). The second coinage gold consists of
(1) the rose-ryal (Fig. 23) (30/-); (2) the spur ryal (Fig. 24)
(15/-); (3) the angel (10/-); (4) the half-angel (5/-); (5) the unite
(20/-); (6) the double crown (10/-); (7) the Britain crown (5/-);
(8) the Thistle crown, a newcomer (4/-) and (9) the half-crown
(2/6). In 1611 the nominal value of all the gold coins was raised
by 2/- in the pound despite the fact their weight had been
reduced. Items 1 to 4 were struck in 'standard' gold and items 5
to 9 in 'crown' gold.

The items of 'standard' gold had the legend A DNO FACTVM EST
ISTVD ET EST MIRAB IN OCVLIS NRIS (This is the work of the Lord
and is wonderful in our eyes) whilst of the 'crown' gold series

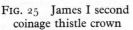

FIG. 25   James I second
coinage thistle crown

FIG. 26   James I second
coinage half-penny

the reverse legend FACIVM EOS IN GENTEM VNAM (I will make them one nation) appeared on the twenty-shilling sovereign now known as a 'unite' to commemorate the Union.

The smaller gold coins had the reverse legend HENRICVS ROSAS REGNA IACOBVS (Henry [united] the roses, James [united] the realm). The thistle crown (a new gold coin) (Fig. 25) has a crowned rose on the obverse and a crowned thistle on the reverse with the TVEATVR legend.

The second coinage silver crowns, shillings and sixpences are similar to the first coinage but the reverse legend is QVAE DEVS CONIVNXIT NEMO SEPARET (What God has joined together let no man put asunder) and the obverse MAG' BRIT' FRAN' or abbreviations thereof.

The thistle and crown, featured on the new small gold four-shilling piece, appear again on the small denominations of the second coinage silver, i.e. the half-groat, penny and half-penny (Fig. 26). In 1619 a third gold coinage was introduced and it was again decided to reduce the weight. All the gold coins of the third coinage had new designs. The twenty-shilling piece (known as a laurel) (Fig. 28) bore a Roman style bust of the King i.e. laureated, cuirassed and draped. The reverse of the rose ryal (upon which the Tudor rose and shield were formerly displayed) now has the royal arms set in a circle of lis, lions and roses with a large xxx (for the value). The fifteen shilling piece (spur ryal) which formerly had the King in ship obverse now has a crowned lion holding a shield and sceptre together with XV.

The angel differs from its predecessors inasmuch as the ship on the reverse is of entirely different style, being a man-of-war

FIG. 27   James I third coinage angel (pierced as touchpiece)

FIG. 28 James I laurel

in full sail (Fig. 27) and not a medieval ship as before. The half-laurel and quarter-laurel have the same Roman-type portrait of the King as the laurel. The half-angel and thistle crown denominations were discontinued.

The third coinage silver of James I is very similar to that of his second coinage but the use of silver mined in Wales was indicated by plumes. After 1621 all crowns (Fig. 29), half-crowns and shillings struck from such silver had the Prince of Wales' plumes over the shield on the reverse.

There was a tremendous outcry, at this time, for small change and the first attempt to introduce a copper coinage was made. James conceived the idea of placing the issue of farthings in the hands of a private person who had to pay for the privilege. He granted a licence to Lord Harrington for the purpose of striking copper farthing tokens. On the death of Lord Harrington the

FIG. 29 James I third coinage crown (plume over shield)

FIG. 30   Harrington farthing

licence was bought by the Duke of Lennox. The new farthing (Fig. 30) bore the King's name and title and had on one side a crown with two crossed sceptres and on the other a crowned harp. The 'Harrington' and 'Lennox' farthings were very unpopular.

The *Scottish* coins of James I first coinage (after his Accession to the English throne) are sometimes confused with his English coins. The Scottish pieces all have the mint mark thistle and the QVAE DEVS legend, and most pieces have & for ET.

Elizabeth 1557-1602

This reign is notable for the variety of denominations issued i.e. nine gold and eleven silver. They are the gold 'fine' sovereign (Fig. 31), the ryal of 15/-, the angel of 10/-, half angel, quarter angel, the 'pound' sovereign of 20/- (Fig. 33), the half-sovereign, gold crown and half-crown, silver crown (Fig. 34) and half-crown, shilling (Fig. 35), sixpence, groat, threepence, half-groat, three-halfpence, penny, three-farthings and half-penny.

The 'fine' sovereign, ryal and angel were of 'standard' gold whilst the sovereign, half-sovereign, crown and half-crowns were of 'crown' gold. Up to this time all the coins had been struck by hand. In Elizabeth's reign the first attempt was made to strike money by a machine. In 1561 Eloi Mestrelle was invited to set up his machine mills at the Tower Mint. The coins produced by him are of much finer workmanship than those made by the hand-hammering method. There was opposition from the mint workers (who feared redundancy) to the introduction of machinery

FIG. 31   Elizabeth I 'fine' sovereign

36

FIG. 32   Elizabeth I milled coinage sixpence

and Mestrelle was eventually discharged, but numerous examples
of his work have survived including 'milled' gold half-pounds,
crowns and half-crowns and silver shillings, sixpences (Fig. 32),
groats, threepences, half-groat (Fig. 38) and three-farthings.
Nearly a hundred years was to pass before the hammered coinage
was finally superseded by the machinery. Mestrelle fell into evil
practices and was hanged at Norwich for making false money.
At the accession of Elizabeth there was a large quantity of the
base money of Edward VI still in circulation, particularly testoons
(shillings). Those of the very worst metal were countermarked
with a greyhound's head and were ordered to be current for $2\frac{1}{2}$d.
Those of somewhat better standard were countermarked with a
portcullis (Fig. 36) and made current for $4\frac{1}{2}$d. In 1561 the base
coinage was demonitised.

The 'fine' sovereigns (Fig. 31) depicted the Queen seated on
the throne, crowned and robed, and holding a sceptre and orb
whilst the reverse bore a square shield bearing the arms of France
and England quarterly on a large double rose—a very handsome
coin. The ryal shows the Queen standing in a ship. The ship has
a high quarterdeck and has a flag at the prow bearing the letter E.
All the other coins have a profile portrait of the Queen on the
obverse, often in a richly embroidered gown. The reverses of the
gold coins (other than the fine sovereign described above) have
the royal arms crowned and the letters ER (Fig. 33); but the
silver has the royal arms superimposed on a cross fourchée
without the crown or initials (Fig. 34).

The legend on the quarter angel is of interest. The obverse

reads ELIZABETH D G ANG FRANCIE and continues on the reverse
ET HIBERNIA REGINA FIDEI. This is the first occasion on which the
title '(Defender) of the Faith' appears on coins of an English
Monarch. Other interesting legends are IHS AVTEM TRANSIENS PER
MEDIVM ILLORVM (But Jesus, passing through the midst of them,
went His way) on the reverse of the ryals; A DNO FACTVM EST
ISTVD, ET EST MIRABILE IN OCVLIS NOSTRIS (This is the work of
the Lord and is wonderful in our eyes) on the reverses of the
'fine' sovereign and the angel and its half, and SCVTVM FIDEI
PROTEGET EAM (the shield of faith protects her) on the 'crown'
gold. The larger silver denominations have POSVI DEVM ADJVTOREM
MEVM (I have made God my helper).

The half-groat and smaller values (Fig. 37) have E' D' G' ROSA
SINE SPINA on the obverse and the mint name CIVITAS LONDON on
the reverse. The half-penny has no inscription, but a portcullis
one side and cross and pellets the other. Roses are found behind
the queen's head on some of the silver coins and are accompanied
by a date on the reverse. Thus we find the shilling with no rose
or date; the sixpence has both; the groat neither; threepence both;
penny neither; three-farthings both. In the last years of the
century patterns were made for a copper coinage but they were
never put into circulation. The reign of Elizabeth offers much
scope to the collector and the smaller coins can still be bought
quite cheaply.

FIG. 33   Elizabeth I 'pound' sovereign

FIG. 34   Elizabeth I crown

FIG. 35   Elizabeth I shilling, early issue

FIG. 36   Devalued Edward VI base shilling
countermarked with portcullis

FIG. 37
Elizabeth I three-farthings

FIG. 38
Elizabeth I milled half-groat

Mary 1553-1554 and Philip and Mary 1554-1558

Mary succeeded to the throne on the death of the young King Edward VI. In 1554 she married Philip of Spain. In the year before her marriage her money was struck in her own name alone. In the next four years her husband's name and sometimes his portrait appear on the coins.

The coinage of her first year consisted of 'fine' sovereigns (Fig. 39), ryals, angels and half-angels (all of which were struck in 'standard' gold); also a great quantity of groats, a few half-groats (Fig. 40) and some pence.

The 'fine' sovereign was a beautiful piece with the Queen seated on a high-backed throne and a portcullis at her feet. The reverse depicted the double Tudor rose with arms in the centre (Fig. 39).

FIG. 39   Mary 'fine' sovereign

The ryal (Fig. 41) shows Mary in a ship carrying a sword in her right hand. This coin is a great rarity. Both sovereign and ryal have as their reverse inscription A DNO' FACTV' EST ISTVD Z EST MIRABIL' IN OCVL' NRV (variously contracted). The date in Roman figures in the obverse legend of the sovereign makes this the first dated English gold coin. The angel has St. Michael and the Dragon on the obverse. On the reverse is a ship, bearing a cross, with the A DNO legend. The half angel is similar and is extremely scarce. The groat bears a flattering portrait of the queen (said to be unlike her actual hard features) as does the half-groat and the 'fine' standard penny. All three have the shield of arms reverse and the legend VERITAS TEMPORIS FILIA (Truth, the daughter of Time).

FIG. 40   Mary half-groat

FIG. 41   Mary ryal

The coins struck before her marriage have the name MARIA or M only on the smaller denominations and many of them have a pomegranate (the badge of her mother, Katherine of Aragon) after the first or second word on the legend.

After her marriage, Mary at once conceded to her husband, not only all regal honours, but also an equal place upon the coinage. The only gold coins struck in their joint names were the angel and half-angel and these were of the same type as before except for the obverse inscription which now reads PHILIP Z MARIA D. G. REX Z REGINA, and P and M on each side of the cross on the reverse. They are both rare.

The silver struck in their joint names consists of the shilling, sixpence, groat, half-groat and penny. The shilling is interesting inasmuch as it is the only coin upon which joint sovereigns are represented face to face. Indeed it gave rise to the following couplet:

'Still amorous, fond and billing,
Like Philip and Mary on a shilling.'

The reverse of this shilling has an oval shield, crowned and garnished, bearing the arms of Philip and Mary impaled, and with X and ii at either side of the crown to denote the value (Fig. 42).

FIG. 42   Philip & Mary shilling

The legend reads POSVIMVS DEVM ADIVTOREM NOSTRVM (We have made God our helper). The sixpences are of the same type. The groats, half-groats and pennies are of the same types as those which were struck before the marriage (portrait of Mary alone) except in having Philip's name (or initial) added to that of Mary. Also the reverse legend of the groat and half-groat reads POSVIMVS etc. instead of VERITAS etc. The pennies, both fine and base (only 4 grains fine) read as before, CIVITAS LONDON.

Edward VI 1547-1553

Edward VI was only nine years old when his father died. His ministers, led by the Duke of Somerset, were responsible for the coinage and it seems that for over a year they continued to use the late King's coin dies. Thus there are few coins of Edward's earliest years as Monarch which show his name. There is a considerable amount of money bearing the name of Henry (VIII), his father, which bear mint marks and portraits which make it fairly certain that they belong to Edward's reign. One series of half-sovereigns bear the name of Henry but the enthroned figure has a youthful face.

In 1547–49 shillings were struck with the youthful Edward's own portrait in profile and crowned.

FIG. 43   Edward VI first period groat

On the reverse is an oval garnished shield with the legend TIMOR DOMINI FONS VITAE (The fear of the Lord is the fountain of life) followed by the date (MDXLVIII) in Roman numerals (similar to Fig. 47). These are the first English coins to bear a date. They were struck in base (half-alloy) silver and in great quantities. Groats (Fig. 43), half-groats and pennies similar in type were also struck but these are rarer. During this reign coins were struck at Southwark, Bristol, Canterbury and York as

well as Tower Mint in London and the newly established mint at
Durham House in the Strand. The shillings described above were
struck at Durham House.

The first issue of gold coins bearing Edward's name consist of
half-sovereigns, crowns and half-crowns. The half-sovereign
shows the King enthroned on the obverse and the royal arms
crowned and supported by a lion and dragon on the reverse.
The legend is the familiar IHS AVTEM etc. The crown (which is
unique) and the half-crown (which is very rare) have a crowned
rose between E & R on the obverse and the reverse has crowned
arms. A distinguishing mark of the first coinage is the numeral
6 after the King's name.

In 1549 the fineness of the gold coins was raised from 20 to 22
carat and coins of this new issue can be recognised by the Roman
numeral VI after the King's name. A full sovereign was now
issued and shows the King crowned and enthroned, drawn
sword in the right hand and orb in the left. The reverse is
similar to that of the half-sovereign of the first issue (arms and
supporters). The half-sovereign, gold crowns and half-crowns
can have either a crowned or uncrowned profile bust, and one
of the following legends TIMOR DOMINE FONS VITE, SCVTVM FIDEI
PROTEGET EVM (The shield of faith shall protect him) or LUCERNA
PEDIBVS MEIS VERBVM TVVM (Thy word is a lantern unto my feet)
on the obverse or the reverse. The obverse of these coins has
an oval shield of arms crowned and garnished with E and R on
either side (Fig. 44).

FIG. 44   Edward VI half-sovereign (second period)

This is the first time that a monarch appears uncrowned on our
coins and they are delightful pieces.

Shillings (Fig. 47) of two different standards were now struck—
a large one weighing 80 grains and a small one of 60 grains. They
both have a crowned profile bust of the King and the date in
Roman figures. Some have the legend INIMICOS EIVS INDVAM
CONFVSIONE (As for His enemies, I shall clothe them with shame).

The smaller shilling of 60 grains (of better silver than the 80
grain shilling) was very unpopular. In 1550 new larger shillings
were issued but they were made of very base silver (i.e. one
quarter silver and threequarters alloy).

In 1551 improvements were made. The silver coinage was
struck from 11 oz. fine silver (11 ozs. silver and one ounce alloy)
and was known as 'fine' silver. Two finenesses of gold were used,
23 carat for the sovereign of 30/- and the angel of 10/-, and 22
carat for the sovereign of 20/- and its parts.

FIG. 45   Edward VI sovereign (third period)

The fine sovereign of 30/- was of the type King enthroned and
royal arms on the Tudor rose. The angel has St. Michael and
the ship. The 20/- sovereign shows an attractive half-length
figure of the King crowned and in armour and bearing a sword
and sceptre (Fig. 45). The half-sovereign, gold crown and gold
half-crown are similar.

With the 'fine' silver issue came the introduction of new
denominations i.e. the crown (Fig. 46) and half-crown which
hitherto had been struck only in gold. These two coins have the
King in armour holding a sword and seated on a horse and the
date, which appears below the horse, is in arabic numerals.

The other denominations struck in 'fine' silver are the shilling (Fig. 49), sixpence and threepence. The sixpence and threepence were making their first appearance. All three have a crowned facing portrait of the King with a rose to the left and the value in Roman numerals to the right.

FIG. 46   Edward VI crown

FIG. 47   Edward VI shilling (second period)

FIG. 48   Edward VI penny of York (base issue)

The smaller denomination continued to be struck in base silver, the farthing being of the portcullis type and the penny (Fig. 48) and half-penny having a large Tudor rose with royal arms on the reverse.

The young King died prematurely at the age of fourteen.

FIG. 49   Edward VI 'fine' shilling

Henry VIII   1509-1547

Henry VIII succeeded to the throne at the age of eighteen. He was the son of Henry VII and Elizabeth of York. He was devoted to enjoying life and for the first fifteen years of his reign was content to retain his father's portrait on his silver coins. His first coinage can only be distinguished from those of Henry VII by the numeral VIII after the King's name in the legend or by the mint marks crowned portcullis and castle.

Between 1526 and 1544 a profile portrait of Henry VIII (Fig. 50) came into use and for the third and last period 1544–49 a facing bust (Fig. 51) of the now ageing monarch was employed (which, incidentally looks extraordinarily like Charles Laughton when he played the part of Henry VIII). In the third issue the Arabic numeral 8 was used instead of the Roman VIII.

Henry VIII's reign is noted for the first tamperings with the purity of the coinage. In 1526 his gold coins started to be made of 22 carat gold followed by yet further debasement of purity and weight. The debasement of silver started in 1543; at first to five parts fine to one of alloy, then to half and half, and finally only one-third silver being used. This was done to provide revenue for the King, who had squandered the fortune left to him by his father, on riotous living. Additional mints were set up at Southwark and Bristol in addition to those at London, Canterbury, York and Durham.

The first coinage included the sovereign (20/-), the angel (6/8d), the half-angel (3/4d), groats, half-groats, 'sovereign' type pennies, half-pennies and farthings. There was no shilling—none was struck until after 1543. Groats and half-groats of London reproduce the portrait and type of Henry VII which we will describe later. The episcopal mints of Canterbury and York

48

were busy. Archbishop Warham (1504–32) struck half-groats (Fig. 52), pennies and half-pennies on a large scale. His pieces are known by the W.A. (Warham Archiepiscopus) on each side of the reverse shield except in the case of the half-pennies when WA appeared by the King's bust.

FIG. 50   Henry VIII second coinage groat

FIG. 51   Henry VIII third coinage shilling

FIG. 52   Henry VIII second coinage half-groat
struck at Canterbury

Archbishop Bainbridge at York (1508–14) started with X and B on each side of the reverse shield, but on being made a Cardinal in 1511 he put a cardinal's hat below the shield on the reverse of his half-groats which were the only denomination issued. Cardinal

D

Wolsey also issued this denomination and these are distinguished by TW on either side of the reverse shield and sometimes the Keys of St. Peter and a cardinal's hat below the shield. The Durham pennies of Bishop Thomas Ruthall have the letters T and D above or beside the royal arms.

All the pence of the first coinage adhere to the type of the seated sovereign introduced on the second coinage of Henry VII. Their only distinguishing mark is the portcullis mint mark, the King's name having no numeral after it. This also applies to the half-pence and farthing. The latter is extremely rare.

Henry's first coinage sovereign shows him seated on the throne with a portcullis at his feet. The reverse has the usual double rose and shield. The angel (Fig. 53) and angelet have the usual archangel Michael standing with both feet on the dragon. The reverse has the ship and arms with H on one side of the mast and a rose on the other, and the legend PER CRVCEM etc. The legend on the angelet is O CRVX, AVE, SPES VNICA (Hail! O cross, the only hope).

The year 1526 saw the introduction of the second coinage. Cardinal Wolsey was Chancellor of the Exchequer and the King commanded him to re-organise the coinage by bringing its standard into line with that of the continental countries. This was done in an effort to stop the importation of French and Flemish gold coins. Accordingly the sovereign became current for 22 shillings and sixpence, the angel for seven and sixpence and the angelet for three and ninepence. A new gold coin, to be called the 'Crown of the Rose' (Fig. 54) was introduced in imitation of the French 'Crown of the Sun' (écu de soleil) and this was made current for four and sixpence. Another new denomination to be introduced was the George noble which was to be current for six and eightpence and a half George noble in proportion. Yet another new denomination to be introduced was called the 'Crown of the Double Rose' to be current for 5/-; and its half for 2/6 (Fig. 55). The crowns and half-crowns were to be made of 22 carat gold and are the first instance of a gold coin of less than standard fineness in England.

FIG. 53   Henry VIII angel

FIG. 54   Henry VIII crown of the rose

FIG. 55   Henry VIII half-crown of the double-rose

In 1540 Henry assumed the title of King of Ireland, but it does not seem to have been adopted on the English coins until 1543. The sovereigns and angels were the same type as before. The George noble had the ship as on the reverse of the angels, but a double rose instead of a shield above it under the cross; H is to the left of the cross, and K (for Katherine of Aragon) to the right. The reverse shows St. George on horseback, piercing the dragon through the mouth. The mint mark is always a rose. The obverse legend reads HENRIC DI G R AGL Z FRANC DNS HIBERNI (Henry, by the grace of God, King of England and France, Lord of Ireland). The reverse legend reads TALI DICA SIGNO MES FLVCTVARI NEQUIT (With such a sign [the cross] a devoted mind is unable to waver). These coins are very rare and must have been struck between 1526 and 1533 when Katherine was divorced.

The 'Crown of the Rose' has the royal arms surmounted by a large crown on the obverse and the reverse has a large rose in the centre of a cross and the legend HENRICVS RVTILANS ROSA SINE SPINA (Henry, the dazzling rose without a thorn). The extremely rare 'crown of the rose' struck in 23 carat gold was replaced by the 'crown of the double rose' and its half, both of which were struck in 22 carat gold. These retain the RVTILAN ROSA legend but on their obverse they have a large Tudor rose surmounted by a crown and both sides of the coin bear the initial of the King's name with that of his queen at the time of their issue; K (Katherine of Aragon); A (Anne Boleyn); or I (Jane Seymour), and sometimes R (Rex).

The King's marriage with Katherine, who was the widow of his brother Arthur, was celebrated in 1509 and was decreed void in 1533. This was shortly *after* the King had announced his marriage to Anne Boleyn which had taken place in November 1532. Anne was beheaded in May 1536 and the day after this event the King married Jane Seymour. Jane gave birth to Edward VI on Oct. 12th 1537 and she died two days later.

In January 1540 the King married Anne of Cleves and by July of the same year he had divorced her. On the 8th August 1540 he married Katherine Howard who was beheaded in January 1542. On the 12th July 1543 he married Katherine Parr, Lady Latimar who outlived him. To return to the coinage—we will now describe the second coinage silver.

The first actual portrait of Henry VIII is found on the groats and half-groats of the second coinage silver coins (Fig. 50). Hitherto, the portrait of his father, Henry VII, had been used. The groats and half-groats struck at York read CIVITAS EBORACI and some half-groats coined at Canterbury read CIVITAS CANTOR. Some rare groats have the obverse inscription ending HIB REX. The penny and half-penny have the flattering legend H. D. G. ROSA SINE SPINA (Henry, by the grace of God, a rose without a thorn). The pennies (Fig. 56) have the 'sovereign' design and on the half-pennies (Fig. 57) the conventional facing head is seen for the last time.

The silver of the second coinage was not debased but the weights of the coins were reduced.

FIG. 56   Henry VIII   FIG. 57   Henry VIII
Canterbury penny   London half-penny

Before proceeding to the last coinage of Henry VIII mention must be made again of the ecclesiastical mints. Henry quarrelled with the Pope and established the Church of England. After this the clergy were not allowed to strike their own coins and the monastries were closed down. The York groats and half-groats of Wolsey and his 'sovereign' type penny of York and Durham have his cardinal's hat placed below the royal arms and the initials TW at the sides of the shield. After Wolsey's fall, his successor at York, Edward Lee issued half-groats with EL. At Durham, Cuthbert Tunstall issued pence with CD (Cuthbert Dunelmensis). At Canterbury, Archbishop Wareham coined half-groats, pennies and half-pennies that bear WA (Wareham Archiepiscopus) (Fig. 56). His successor, Thomas Cranmer issued half-groats, pennies and half-pennies bearing his initials TC.

In 1544 the third coinage was begun and this marked a period of further debasement in the quality of the metal and a great increase in the amount of alloy used. Gold coins were issued of 23, 22 and finally only 20 carat fineness. The silver coins had only one-third silver content, the rest being copper alloy. The gold sovereign (Fig. 58) and half-sovereign have the King seated on his throne with a rose at his feet instead of the portcullis. The reverse shows the royal arms with two supporters. The sovereign became worth 20/– and its weight was reduced. Gold crowns and half-crowns were issued, and angels were issued at 8/– together with half-angels.

The quarter-angel appeared for the first time at a value of 2/–. They were the same type as the full angel. Gold sovereigns, half-sovereigns, gold crowns and half-crowns were also struck at the

Bristol Mint which opened in 1546. These coins have a WS monogram in the legend, being the initials of William Sharington who was in charge. Another mint was also set up at Southwark to speed the production of the coins. They have the mint mark S. On the silver of the third coinage the full face bust appears—the King is now bearded and middle-aged. The third coinage silver consisted of testoons, groats, half-groats, pennies and half-pennies. The obverse of the testoon (which had not hitherto been issued by Henry VIII) has the crowned full-face bust, with beard and wearing a mantle and fur collar. The reverse shows a double rose surmounted by a crown with H and R crowned. The legend is POSVI DEVM ADIVTORIVM MEVM (I have made God my helper) or a variation.

FIG. 58   Henry VIII 3rd coinage sovereign

The groat, half-groat and penny have the same obverse as the testoon but their reverses are similar to the earlier pieces (i.e. shield). Some rare groats and half-groats of the last issue have the reverse legend REDDE CVIQVE QVOD SVVM EST (Render to every man that which is his own). Silver coins were struck at London in the Tower, Southwark and at provincial mints opened at Bristol, Canterbury and York to supplement the output. Towards the end of Henry VIII's reign the medieval Lombardic lettering was replaced by Roman lettering. Henry died in 1547 but the base gold and silver coins continued to be struck with his name and portrait for the next four years.

Henry VII 1485-1509

To Henry VII we owe the introduction of the first sovereign and the silver testoon (or shilling). The name testoon was taken from that of the first French coin bearing the head of the King (in place of the stereotyped symbolical bust that had previously been used on medieval coins) and known as a teste (tête). These two coins were struck in addition to the rose noble (or ryal), angel, angelet, groat, half-groat, penny, half-penny and farthing. The sovereign was a magnificent piece and was worth twenty shillings. This depicted the full length figure of the King seated on an elaborate throne holding orb and sceptre and the field covered with fleur-de-lis. The reverse shows a large Tudor double rose with the royal arms in the centre. The double rose signified the union of the Houses of York and Lancaster by the marriage of Henry VII (a Lancastrian) to the Yorkist Princess Elizabeth.

The ryal of this reign is a great rarity. It has the obverse showing the King in armour standing in a ship and holding a sword and shield. A flag to his right bears a dragon and one to his left the initial H. The reverse bears the arms of France alone. This is difficult to explain but it may refer to Henry's pretentions to the French throne. The angel, the commonest of Henry's gold coins, was modified in 1495 when the medieval feathered St. Michael was replaced by a finer archangel clothed in tight-fitting chain mail. He stands with both feet on the dragon (not with one only as in previous issues). (Fig. 59).

The influence of the Renaissance was beginning to show itself. With the exception of the ryal the output of gold was large—a sign that England was flourishing.

The silver coinage of this reign is very interesting. Since the reign of Edward III the coins had undergone little change and

FIG. 59   Henry VII angel

in the early years of the reign they still retained the conventional facing portrait (Fig. 60) and cross and pellets reverse. An artistic portrait was now adopted for the silver coinage.

FIG. 60   Henry VII facing bust issue groat

FIG. 61   Henry VII profile issue groat

Alexander de Brugsal, the chief engraver at the mint was responsible for the fine profile head of Henry VII on the groats (Fig. 61) and on the newly introduced testoons already referred to. These were the first coins to be struck with a profile portrait (in this country) since the reign of Stephen. The reverses are changed to the royal arms superimposed on a long cross. The profile coins have VII after the King's name and some very rare testoons read HENRIC SEPTIM.

The gold coins, groats and half-groats were struck only in London. Half-groats (Fig. 62) were struck at Canterbury and at the ecclesiastical mint of York.

FIG. 62   Henry VII Canterbury half-groat

'Sovereign' type pennies were struck at London (Fig. 63) and were also struck for Archbishop Rotherham of York (with the Keys of St. Peter's below the shield on the reverse); for Bishop Sherwood of Durham (with a crozier and the letters D and S at the sides of the shield). At York a mint was opened for coining half-groats and these have a lozenge shaped panel in the centre of the reverse cross.

The coins of Henry VII are considered to demonstrate the transition between medieval and Renaissance art.

FIG. 63   Henry VII sovereign type penny of London

Edward V 1483 and Richard III 1483-1485

The coins of Edward V and Richard III are alike except that they read Edward and Richard respectively. Edward V was the eldest of the two young sons of Edward IV known to posterity as the 'Princes in the Tower'. He reigned for less than eleven weeks under the guardianship of his wicked uncle Richard, Duke of Gloucester. That unscrupulous gentleman had his nephews imprisoned in the Tower and they were later murdered there.

Before Richard of Gloucester seized the Protectorship of the realm on 4th May, 1483 angels, half-angels, groats (Fig. 64), half-groats and pennies were struck bearing the halved sun and rose mintmark and the name Edward. During the period Richard claimed to be Protector (not King) he changed the obverse mintmark to a boar's head (his own badge) but let the rose and sun remain unaltered of the reverse. This period lasted less than seven weeks i.e. 7th May to 26th June, 1483. On the assassination of his nephews Richard seized the crown, and the coins ceased to be issued in Edward's name. The coins of Richard were angels (Fig. 66), half-angels, groats (Fig. 65), half-groats, pennies and half-pennies and excepting for the change in the name all these pieces are of the same design, weight and fineness and bear the same marks as those of the ill-fated Edward V (in fact similar to the last coinage of Edward IV which we will examine carefully in a later chapter). Archbishop Rotherham struck pennies at York and they have a T and Key by the King's bust (Fig. 67). Bishop Sherwood also struck pennies at Durham and these have an S on the King's neck and a D in the centre of the reverse. Mintmarks had by now come into general use. They were placed at the beginning of the legend on either or both sides of the coins. They help the collector to distinguish the various issues, and

58

often to date them accurately. In 1485, Richard's brief and rather violent reign ended with his death (at the hands of Henry Tudor, Earl of Richmond) on the field of Bosworth. The death of Richard III tends to mark the end of medieval art in our coinage. Most of the coins of Edward V and Richard III are rare.

FIG. 64   Edward IV/V groat

FIG. 65   Richard III groat of London

FIG. 66   Richard III angel

FIG. 67   Richard III York penny with T and key

Henry VI 1422-1461, Edward IV 1461-1483, Henry VI restored 1470-1471 and Edward IV, 2nd. reign, 1471-1483

The infant Henry VI succeeded his father, Henry V. The coins of this reign can be divided into eleven periods according to their symbols (or privy marks), the use of which was beginning to be developed. These marks are found either in the field of the coin or they are used as stops in the legend. The eleven periods are as follows:—

Annulet	**O**	= 1422–1427
Rosette-Mascle	❀◊	= 1427–1430
Pinecone-Mascle	◊	= 1430–1434
Leaf-Mascle	◊	= 1434–1435
Leaf-Trefoil	∴	= 1435–1438
Trefoil	∴	= 1438–1443
Trefoil-Pellet	∴ •	= 1443–1445
Leaf-Pellet	•	= 1445–1454
Unmarked		= 1453–1454
Cross-Pellet	**X** •	= 1454–1460
Lis-Pellet	⚜ •	= 1456–1460

Until the beginning of this reign, the commencement of legends had been marked by a plain cross but now various kinds of cross (i.e. cross pommée, cross patonce, cross fleurée and voided cross) came into use on the silver coins, but the gold coins have a fleur-de-lis as a reverse mintmark. The archbishops of York and bishops of Durham were very busy during this reign. Their personal marks were placed upon their coins i.e. the pennies of York have a quatrefoil in the centre of the reverse; some of the pennies of Durham have two-interlinked rings on the reverse; and later the letter B (Laurence Booth) appears by the King's neck.

Henry VI struck nobles (Fig. 68), half-nobles and quarter-nobles at London, Calais and York. Some of the gold coins of Calais can be distinguished by a flag flying at the stern of the ship and some have a C in the centre of the reverse. The York issue of nobles and half-nobles of 1422 have a large lis in the field of the obverse, above the stern of the ship. The quarter-noble of York has two lis over the shield.

Of the silver coins, groats (Figs. 69 and 70), half-groats (Fig. 71), pennies (Fig. 72), half-pennies and farthings (Fig. 73) were struck, a large amount of which were coined at Calais. This

FIG. 68   Henry VI noble, 'annulet' issue

FIG. 69   Henry VI groat, 'annulet' issue

FIG. 70   Henry VI rosette mascle issue Calais groat

mint was closed in 1440 and no English coins were struck in
France again. A groat of Calais of the 'annulet' issue is one of
the most common of all English medieval coins (Fig. 69).

The struggle between the Houses of Lancaster and York is
known as The War of the Roses. From this time onwards the
rose became a familiar feature of the coinage. The Lancastrian
army was defeated by the Yorkists at the battle of Wakefield in
1460. Henry VI was imprisoned in the Tower, where he languished
for the next nine years and Edward of York on reaching London
was acclaimed King Edward IV. Henry VI and Edward IV were
both destined to have two separate reigns each.

FIG. 71   Henry VI York half-groat, 'annulet' issue

FIG. 72   Henry VI Calais penny, pinecone mascle issue

FIG. 73   Henry VI London farthing, pinecone mascle issue

On his accession Edward IV continued to strike coins of the same type as his predecessor. The gold coins are distinguishable by reason of the fact that the legend commences at the top left (11 o'clock) instead of top right (1 o'clock) as previously. These are extremely rare.

In 1464 a change took place. To establish a better ratio between gold and silver the weight of the penny was reduced from 15 to 12 grains. Other denominations were reduced in proportion and a year later a new gold coin was introduced called a rose-noble or ryal (royal) (Fig. 74).

This coin weighed 120 grains (instead of 108 grains as previously) and was valued at ten shillings (instead of 6/8d) with the half and quarter in proportion. The new noble had a large Yorkist rose on the side of the ship and a banner with E on it appeared at the stern. The rose superimposed on a sun appears again in

FIG. 74   Edward IV rose noble or ryal

FIG. 74A   Edward IV angel, second reign

the centre of the obverse. The reverse legend is the familiar IHC AUTEM etc. with variations.

To help with the production of the new coins several provincial mints were brought into use i.e. Bristol, Coventry, Norwich and York. Coins from these mints have the letters B, C, N or E (Eboracum = York) placed in waves under the ship. Coventry and Norwich mints were closed down after two months, York continued until September 1471 and Bristol until July 1472.

The old noble of 6/8d was greatly missed as this sum had become the standard professional fee. This was the reason for the introduction of another new denomination in gold—the angel of 6/8d and the half-angel of 3/4d. They were smaller than the old noble. The obverse of the angel depicts St. Michael (as an angel) slaying the dragon and the reverse has a ship carrying the royal arms surmounted by a cross and sun in splendour; on either side of the cross are a small sun and rose. The King (on the older nobles) has now disappeared. The reverse legend reads PER CRVCEM TVAM SALVA NOS XPC REDEMPTOR (By Thy Cross save us, O Christ our Redeemer).

Later the angels change slightly on the reverse inasmuch as there is a letter E instead of a sun at the side of the cross and no sun over the cross. The half-angels are similar to the later angels although the ship became the obverse, and the reverse legend reads O CRVX AVE SPEC VNICA (Hail, O Cross, our only hope). The angel gradually superseded the rose-noble which was not very popular in this country although it found favour on the Continent where it was copied by the Dukes of Burgundy (the rulers of Flanders) and others.

The silver coins of Edward IV were struck at London (Fig. 75), Norwich, York (Fig. 77), Canterbury, Coventry and Bristol (Fig. 78). Groats of London are the commonest of Edward's coins. The provincial groats have the initial letter of the mint on the King's breast and the full mint name on the reverse.

Mention must be made of the issues from the ecclesiastical mints of Canterbury, Durham and York. The Archbishop of Canterbury had the right to coin, given to him in 1465. He struck groats and half-groats, pence and half-pence bearing his distinguishing mark—a knot (below the King's bust) and an archbishop's pall (as mintmark).

FIG. 75   Edward IV first reign heavy groat, London

FIG. 76   Edward IV first reign heavy half-groat, London

Most of the coins issued by the clergy bear their initials i.e.
G for George Neville at York on his pence; B or D for Bishop
Booth at Durham etc. The regular use of mintmarks began in
this reign.

In 1470, under the auspices of Lord Warwick, Henry VI
emerged from prison, was restored to the throne and remained
in power from October 1470 until April 1471. Coining began
promptly at London, Bristol and York.

FIG. 77   Edward IV first reign light groat, York
E on breast

Except for the change of name, Henry's coins of the Restoration
period are similar to those of Edward IV. The same denominations
were struck—all the silver, from groats to farthings, together with

E

FIG. 78   Edward IV first reign light groat, Bristol
B on breast

FIG. 79   Edward IV first reign light half-penny, London

angels and half-angels (which were the only type of gold coins struck until the reign of Henry VIII). New mint marks came into use and also an H replaced the sun on one side of the mast of the ship on the reverse of the angels and a lis replaced the Edwardian rose on the other side of the mast.

During the six and half-months of the restoration of Henry VI, Edward IV had been plotting for his return to the throne. On 11 April, 1471, after a well planned campaign, he seized London. Henry was again committed to the Tower where he was murdered and Edward had another 12 years' sovereignty before him.

The coinage of Edward's second reign is similar to that of his first except that angels (Fig. 74A) and angelets were the only gold coins to be struck. These coins differ from those of his first reign by having an E and a rose on each side of the mast on the reverse (instead of a sun and a rose) and they seem to be less well-executed than the original angels. We have already mentioned in an earlier chapter that angels are often found with a hole punched through them for use as 'touch pieces'.

The same silver denominations as those of the Restoration period were struck and there were also large issues from the ecclesiastical mints of York and Durham. They can be distinguished from the coins of Edward's first reign by their mint-marks. Edward IV died on 9th April, 1483.

Henry V 1413-1422

Henry V coined the same denominations as Henry VI. No numerals in the legends distinguished one Henry from the other. This can be done by close study of detail of type, the legends and the style of the lettering. Unfortunately, space does not allow us to examine these problems closely. However, during this reign, a cross with a pellet in the centre, and later a pierced cross, marked the beginning of the obverse legend. Privy marks such as a mullet (five pointed star), a broken annulet or a trefoil appear on most of Henry V coins (except the last issue, when most marks were removed). There is a tendency for the coins of Henry V to be of rather poor workmanship, the letters of the legends being badly formed. The Calais mint was not in use during the reign of Henry V and coins were mostly struck at Durham, London and York.

The mullet is found in different places in the various denominations. On the noble (Fig. 80), below the King's sword arm; on the half-noble above the right top corner of his shield; on the quarter-noble on the right side of the shield on the reverse; on

FIG. 80   Henry V noble, mullet below King's sword arm

the groat and half-groat on the King's breast; on the penny it is displayed prominently in the field of the obverse.

The broken annulet mark came later. On nobles and half-nobles it appears on the side of the ship and sometimes in the quarters on the reverse. On quarter-nobles and pennies it is found at the side of the shield in the former, and the side of the King's head in the latter. On the half-groats it appears at the top of the coin to the left of the King's crown.

The trefoil mark (three pellets) can be found on the obverse, the reverse, or both. On the noble and the half-noble the trefoil is sometimes found between the King's shield and the prow of the ship; sometimes on the side of the ship and sometimes in the quarters on the reverse. On the quarter-noble it appears at the side of the obverse shield. On the half-groat it is found at the side of the King's crown on the obverse. On the penny the King has a mullet to the left and a trefoil to the right. On the next series of this reign the distinguishing mark is two annulets and on the silver coins it turns up on the reverse with one annulet inserted in the inscription and the other in one of the quarters. The noble of this series has annulet stops between each word of the legends, except for a mullet after HENRIC on the obverse and after IHS on the reverse. A new portrait was in use now. This introduced a new feature in the King's appearance i.e. side-locks. These are tufts of hair protruding just below (Fig. 81) the crown and they continue to appear until a profile portrait was introduced on the silver coins of Henry VII. Though he reigned for nine years only, the coins of Henry V are not uncommon. It should be mentioned that ecclesiastical mints of York and Durham struck pennies during this reign.

FIG. 81   Henry V groat, mullet on breast

Henry IV 1399-1413

At the beginning of this reign the economic state of the country was bad. The gold coins were undervalued in relation to foreign coins. So in 1412 the noble was reduced to 108 grains instead of 120 (the previous standard) and the penny from 18 grains to 15 grains. Other denominations were reduced in proportion but all the values were retained. This established a more satisfactory ratio of 11 to 1 between silver and gold, instead of the 12 to 1 ratio which had prevailed since 1351. It also made it unprofitable to export bullion to the Continent. Henry IV coins are divided into heavy and light issues. Heavy coinage nobles, half-nobles and quarter-nobles, half-groats, pence (Fig. 82), half-pence and farthings were struck but no heavy coinage groats are known. The symbols crescent, coronet, star and pellet distinguish the heavy coins. The Archbishop of York struck pennies of this coinage. Heavy coinage was struck from 1399 to 1412.

The light coinage was introduced in 1412 but Henry died in 1413. The light coinage bears the symbols trefoil, annulet and pellet. Nobles of the light coinage have a trefoil and an annulet on the ship's side and a trefoil in one quarter of the reverse and the half-nobles are similar.

The groats, half-groats and pennies struck at London all have an annulet and pellet near the King's crown. Half-pennies

FIG. 82   Henry IV heavy coinage, London penny

69

and farthings of the light coinage were also struck. On most of the coins of this reign the side-locks of hair are absent on the King's portrait.

At this time Charles V occupied the throne of France. He had changed the arms of France from a semée (four or more) of fleur-de-lis to three fleur-de-lis. Henry IV made the same change halfway through his reign. The coins of Henry IV are the scarcest of any from Edward III to the present day (with the exception of those of Edward V) and the heavy coins are rarer than the light. The coins of this reign struck at London are distinguished by a cross pattée mintmark, whilst the half- and quarter-nobles struck at Calais have the mintmark crown.

Richard II   1377-1399

Richard was a boy of ten when he came to the throne where he
was to remain for twenty-two years. He was the son of the Black
Prince (who died in 1376) and grandson of Edward III. No
change was made in the type of the coinage and Richard's coins
had the same indifferent portrait which had served for his grandfather, although the head and style of lettering was altered towards
the end of the reign. Other respects in which the coins differ,
is that they have Richard's name in the obverse legend and R
instead of E or L in the centre of the reverse on the nobles and
half-nobles. Also, with the developing use of privy marks, symbols,
such as a lion, an escallop or a crescent, were placed on the rudder
of the ship on some nobles and half-nobles, to distinguish the
different periods of issue. The noble (Fig. 83) weighed 120 grains
and was current for 6/8d with the other gold coins in proportion.
The same gold and silver coins, excepting the florin and its half
and quarter, which never appeared again, were issued by Richard
II as by his grandfather and these will be described in full in the
next chapter. In 1399 Richard was dethroned by Henry of
Hereford. Henry was proclaimed King and Richard died in prison.

FIG. 83   Richard II noble

71

The commonest and cheapest coins of this reign are the half-pennies struck at London (Fig. 84).

FIG. 84   Richard II London half-penny

FIG. 85   Richard II groat

FIG. 86   Richard II London penny

Edward III 1327-1377

Edward III coined groats, half-groats, pennies, half-pennies and farthings in silver together with six denominations in gold namely the florin, half-florin, quarter-florin, noble, half-noble and quarter-noble. With the exception of the florin and its parts these denominations continued to be struck by each succeeding monarch until late in the reign of Henry VII. Differences in style and weight throughout these long years were slight and have been noted in preceding chapters which will become clearer if we now examine the coin types of Edward III carefully.

In 1344 an effort was made to introduce a gold coinage. There was a tremendous need for a coin larger than a silver penny in order to facilitate trade with European countries which already had a gold currency i.e. North Italy, France and Flanders. Accordingly, the florin (or double-leopard), half-florin (or leopard) and quarter-florin (or helm) were struck. The florin (Fig. 87) was current at 6/-. It weighed 108 grains and was of the fineness 23 carats $3\frac{1}{2}$ grains pure gold to $\frac{1}{2}$ grain alloy. This was to be the standard of fineness of all the gold coins until 1526 when, as we have seen, Henry VIII began to tamper with it. The obverse of the florin depicts Edward III, crowned and robed, sitting under a canopy, holding a sceptre in his right hand, and the orb in his left; two leopards are placed one on each side of the throne and fleur-de-lis are sprinkled over the field. The legend reads EDWR○D○GRA REX○ANGL○Z○FRANC○DNS○HIB. The reverse shows a tressure of four curves, with a beaded interior, containing a short beaded cross with quatrefoiled and foliated ends and a quatrefoil in the centre. In each curve of the tressure is a crown and outside each angle of the tressure is a lion or

leopard. The reverse legend reads

ˣ IHCˣ TRANSIENS ˣ PE ˣ MEDIVM ˣ ILLORVM ˣ IBAT

FIG. 87   Edward III florin

The half-florin (Fig. 88) was current at 3/-. The obverse
shows a leopard crowned, and a banner bearing the arms of
France and England is fastened to his neck. The legend is the
same as that of the florin. The reverse is very similar to that of
the florin but the legend is different:

˳DOMINE˳NE˳IN˳FVRORE˳TVO˳ARGVAS˳ME

The quarter-florin (Fig. 89) was current at 1/6d, and its obverse

FIG. 88   Edward III half-florin

FIG. 89   Edward III quarter-florin

shows a lion crowned standing on a helmet, the field being
covered with fleur-de-lis. The reverse shows a short cross potent

on a beaded cross with foliated ends and a quatrefoil in the centre
with the legend EXALTABITVR°IN°GLORIA°

These three coins, which are excessively rare, were not a success
owing to the fact that they were valued too high in proportion
to the silver and in the same year that they were introduced,
they were superseded by two new coins, the noble and quarter-
noble. The noble (Fig. 90) was current for 6/8d and weighed
136·7 grains whilst the quarter-noble was current for 1/8d and
weighed 34·2 grains (approx.).

These very attractive coins depict the King, crowned and in
armour, standing in a ship, with his sword in his right hand,
and a shield bearing the quartered arms of England and France
in his left hand, and the legend:

EDWAR×D×GRA×REX×ANGL×Z×FRANC×DNS×HYB. This design was
received favourably (despite the King being nearly as large as
the ship) and continued in use until the reign of James I.

FIG. 90   Edward III noble

FIG. 91   Edward III quarter-noble (Treaty period)

The quarter-noble (Fig. 91) obverse has a shield with the
arms of France and England quarterly. This is within a double

tressure of six arches, with a trefoil in each spandril and a pellet in each angle.

In 1346 the noble was reduced to 128 grains and a half-noble was struck—the same type of the noble.

In 1351 the weight of the gold coins was still further reduced—the noble now weighing only 120 grains. Despite the reduction in weight they retained the same values (6/8d and proportionately).

The gold coins of the fourth coinage (1351–77) divide into three periods; from 1351 to 1361 during which time the title King of France appears on the coins; from 1361 to 1369 when, in accordance with the terms of the Treaty of Bretigny, the title Lord of Aquitaine was substituted for King of France; and from 1369 to the King's death in 1377 when both titles were used—the treaty of Bretigny having been broken by Charles V of France. A mint was established at Calais for the purpose of recoining continental currency into English money. Many of the gold coins of the Calais mint have a flag at the stern of the ship and some have c in the centre of the reverse.

The first silver coins of Edward III were pennies, half-pennies and farthings. In the year 1351 silver coins of a larger denomination than the penny were introduced i.e. the groat, (fourpence) and half-groat (twopence).

FIG. 92   Edward III groat, Pre-Treaty

FIG. 93   Edward III half-groat, Treaty period

FIG. 94   Edward III penny of London, Pre-Treaty

FIG. 95   Edward III half-penny

FIG. 96   Edward III farthing

Apart from reductions in weight and the opening and closing of some of the provincial mints, these denominations continued to be struck by each monarch succeeding Edward III until late in the reign of Henry VII. The busts of the various Kings remained substantially the same with small differences in style. The chief change was the high-arched crown introduced by Henry VII prior to the appearance of his new profile portrait coins (Fig. 61). The silver coins break up into Pre-Treaty, Treaty and Post-Treaty periods in the same way as the gold. There is one rare groat which bears all four titles: England, France, Aquitaine and Ireland. The penny varied in weight from 22-2/9 grains to 18 grains, the last weight being in use from 1351. The custom, introduced by Edward I, of permitting the ecclesiastical mints to strike coins continued during the reign of Edward III. Pennies of York and Durham have quatrefoils or croziers on the reverse.

The obverse of the groat (Fig. 92) shows the King's bust full face, crowned, and with bare shoulders within a tressure of nine arches and the legend reads: EDWARD. D. G. REX ANGL. Z. FRANC. D. HY.

(or HYB.). The reverse has a long cross with pellets in the angles. The reverse legend is in two circles; in the inner, the town name CIVITAS LONDON (or EBORACI) and in the outer, the motto POSVI DEVM ADIVTOREM MEV (or MEVM). The half-groat (Fig. 93) is similar to the groat.

The penny (Fig. 94) also has the full face bust, crowned and with bare shoulders but it is without the tressure. The reverse of the penny has the cross and pellets but a single circle with the town name. The half-penny (Fig. 95) and farthing (Fig. 96) are similar with slight variations in the legends.

The description of the silver coins of Edward III completes this introduction to the hammered coinage. It is, of course, only a glimpse at some of the more important aspects of the period covered and more detailed accounts can be found elsewhere.

The earliest of the hammered coins struck in Britain may be covered by another volume at a later date.

Stanmore, 1967